Acknowledgements

Our thanks are due to three special people, without whom, this book would not have been possible.

Jackie Piper, Amy's art tutor, for her inspiration and encouragement.
Lesley Maynerd, for the beautiful ministry of the Oak House Quiet Garden, which was the setting of so much of Margaret's work.

We would also like to thank Caroline Vermeulen for her patience and the many hours of painstaking work spent on the layout and design of this book.

Dedication

This book is dedicated to all those who look for shafts of light in dark times.

GU00720458

The Gardener

Drawn by the Gardener
To this quiet place
He bade me rest,
While he revealed the sacred secrets of his love.

Passing beneath the arched cathedraled canopies of green
I stepped into a cloister of fragrance.
A place of wonderful and diverse harmony
Cultivated by his skilled and patient hands.

There blooms of profuse palette,
Coaxed by the warmth and radiance of his love
Unfurled their soft petals
Allowing Him to penetrate their tender hearts
To work his resurrection mystery preparing
New seeds of faith.

Bees hymned the air,
Fed by the nectar of his fragrant labours
While birds winged above me
Pouring into the stillness
The gospels of their secret joys.

Across the garden, the Gardener's presence rippled.
Flowers and tendrils nodded their reverences
And above me the foliage stirred
In cadences of leaf whispering praise.
While my spirit danced across the green sward
to the beat of the Gardener's heart.

MT. June 2004

God with me

Easing myself into stillness
I wait on God in peaceful attention
so that we can be quietly busy.
The light breeze brushes my face
And stirs the branches into a graceful sway.
Tantalising garden scents waft and wane
On the breeze's pulse
As a gnat cloud dances over the pond.

God with me. God stirs me.

In a communion of silence and sound
The carol of running water stills my mind
Collared doves coo and the trill, still songs of blackbirds
Rinse the air as they shadow flit across the garden.

God with me. God speaks.

Farther off the traffic rumbles and planes and distant trains
Carry the unseen, unknown companions of this moment.

God with me. God moves

Lifting my face the sun eases the furrows of my forehead
While God and I review the furrows I have ploughed,
Once seeming straight and well intentioned,
But looking back… criss-crossed.

God with me. God's hand on mine.

MT. April 2004

4

Before the Fire

As I sat before the fire
Safe in its warmth,
Its light played softly across my closed eyelids.
And in the warmth, the movement of its flames lapped
Gently at the corners of my mind,
Until I heard their flickering tongues
Speak in God's voice.

They spoke of rest, warmth and security,
Freeing my frozen thoughts
and melting the fears I had carried,
like cold sharp icicles in my mind.

The dance of the flames drew me close,
Bidding me put down all I carried
And move with them till their lightness
Filled my soul and I was one with them,
Encircled and protected
Basking in the smile of God,
My fragile flame delighting him.

MT. December 2002

Next Year's Poppies

Treading cautiously
Over the leaf clinging slippery stones
The dark figure brooded
Hunched and bowed
Cloaked in the burdens of the year.
Through the toe-numbing, nose-pinching dampness
of the grey morning
it stepped onto the grass.

Wet, autumn-forgotten leaves
Clung to its feet,
To be carried, like the debris of the year.
The broken dreams, the dead embers of anger,
The bitterness of hopes dashed
That swathed the figure
Layer upon layer
Slowing its steps
Lowering its horizons.

Pausing, its glance was arrested
By the incongruous shoots of next year's poppies,
Curling defiantly through the dead shroud of the garden.

And in the distance
Though the misted panes
The small soft orbs of light
Promised a flickering glimpse of the son king.

Doubts rolled uneasily around the edges of the mind
Three fragile flames
Enough to light and lighten such dark heaviness?
Enough to thaw such icy grief?
"We beg to differ", sang the flames
And the darkness could not overcome them.

MT. December 2004

6

The Open Wound

Last night I woke and felt the pain of others.
Their wounds raw and bleeding were there to see…
Their broken-ness a bleeding mess.
No comfort could they find.
No peace, no soothing touch would they allow.
Deep in the wounds were grains of dust and grit.
Stay still…
to move would cause more pain.
I do not dare to touch
but Jesus can.
Open your wounded self and soul to Him.
He knows the pain…He suffered too.
The one He loves is YOU.
Offer Him your broken-ness.
Show Him your wounds,
open , bleeding, bruised and sore
ingrained with dirt and grit,
self –justification, anger, pride, deep hurt.
Stay still…
and offer Him the whole of it.
He knows the broken-ness and pain
The devastation and the loss
His are the healing hands…
hands wounded on the Cross.

AKP. November 1992

Besieging Spirit

I built a wall of worry round my heart
Each stone a testament of care,
Anxieties for those I loved,
Fears for their future and for mine,
Frustrated hopes and shattered dreams
Loomed over and imprisoned me.

Each day, I prayerfully polished every stone
Rehearsed them in constricted anger to my God.
Pleading for this masonry of suffering to fall
So those trapped by their circumstances could find release.

Till angry and exhausted, I could plead no more
And falling back on prayers of occupation
Gazed void and voiceless to the sky.
All supplication spent.

And finding no resistance, then He came
And drenched my soul with rays of dazzling peace.
Detached me, bruised and bleeding from the wreckage of past prayers
To find solace and serenity of hope
And glimpse with Him the beautiful and limitless possibilities
of life shared with a suffering Lord.

MT. July 2004

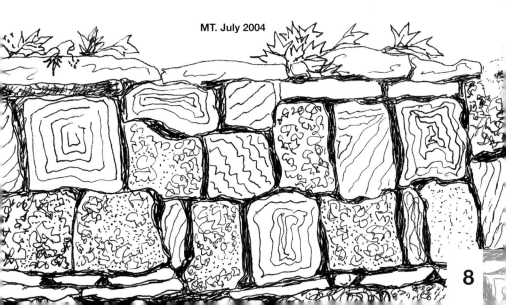

Hollow

Pacing the dark corridor of pain
where no light penetrates,
I reach the farthest door
and enter.
I do my work, anaesthetised by duty
until, with energy spent
I am released
to journey home.

I pass the dark closed doors.
Wooden eyes, firmly shut
against my plight.
Indifferent to my existence.

Occasionally a faint plea causes me to pause.
Feet shifting in fatigue,
I stand and listen
to other whispers of trapped pain,
and I respond,
with murmurs of empty ineffective comfort.

No light illuminates my way.
No chink of opportunity
beckons or diverts my long return.

Destination reached.
the door opens
and swallows me into the limbo of waiting,
with soulless tasks and obligations to fulfil.

The clock ticks.
Time passes
and when it has run its course,
it spits me out to travel on the treadmill path
of hollow giving.

MT. December 2005

A Psalm for Today

I will stand on the rock
Let it rain !
Let the arrows, sticks and stones
rain down on me !
I will stand firm
and wait…

The Lord is near.
He will not let me be washed away.
As long as I live
I will look to him.
When I am weak
I will not give in completely.
My trust is in the Lord.

He has saved me before
and he will do it again.
I have heard his voice
and I will hear it again.

I will not give way
to despair.
I will not move
from my trust
in the Lord.
I will bear
the onslaught
of the storm.
I will be faithful
in prayer
As the Lord
has requested…
The devil is not
going to win !

AKP. December 1995

12

In Intensive Care

I see a body lying there, pale and cold but still alive
– but barely so –
– no movement but a beating heart and gently heaving chest…
But where is his soul?

Lord as your servants so skilled in tending to the flesh
move around with watchful eyes and ministering hands….
Where is his soul?

Lord, as his loved ones come and go, sit or stand, touch him
And speak soft words and pray to you…
Where is his soul?

Lord at times he lies so quiet… at others in distress…
As he is being tended to his agitation rises… another crisis….
But where is his soul?

Does it lie sleeping somewhere deep inside or like a hibernating moth
Is still and quiet in a secret place against a wall?
Where is his soul?

Lord we watch and pray. We, on the side lines,
know the battle rages from side to side.
We have quiet hope despite the war.
But where is his soul?

Lord with your Grace we will continue to support and pray…
And listen too…ready to answer from you a whispered word.
But where is his soul?

Lord, I see a body there and only LIGHT.
High in the corners of the room the angels sing
And in your safe and gentle care… I know not where…
is his soul.

AKP. August 1995

Watch and Pray

What can we do but watch and pray.
Can we do that?
Or like his friends do fail to watch- but sleep.
What can we do?
WATCH and PRAY.
Can we stand firm and watch and pray
through our friend's Gethsemane?
Can we stay still and watch and pray
whilst our friend suffers every day?
Can we forget our loss
and watch and pray beneath the Cross?
Or are we like his friends… we turn away
we cannot bear to stay
and watch and pray?
Can we stay long hours beneath the Cross
until our friend has gone beyond death's gate?
Can we stand firm, faithful and true?
With God's help we can and do.
Then we too can share the Easter joy
And see our risen friend and say
"There is no end!"

A Post-script
For all of us who fail to keep watch
… but fall asleep!

He loves us though we do not watch and pray.
He loves us though we do not stay.
He gives and forgives
and there is no end
to the love we have
from our dear Friend
Jesus Christ our Lord.

AKP. August 1991

16

17

After the Rain

Stay here and watch a while.
Rest in the stillness of the rain-soaked garden,
while the rising breeze ripples though memories of His passion,
stirring the willow fronds to scourge the air with tender green blows.
The holly trembles; its spikes an evergreen echo
of the piercing thorns.
Naked branches thrust their hard and searching fingers to the sky.
Fingers that probed, ripped, stripped,
nailed and hammered.
Beaten by the pitiless lash of stinging rain,
the daffodils, heavy headed,
bend their bedraggled beauty to the earth.

And so I sit and wait and watch,
while distant traffic heedlessly rumbles those who cannot
stay a while, to other destinations.
And fresh arrived upon the scene a scampering squirrel
and a darting blackbird,
with keener eyes than mine and thoughts more innocent,
see only signs of resurrection.

MT. Easter 2005

Jesus, Jesus, Jesus

Say it quietly and with love
It's like the rousing feathers of a dove.

Jesus, Jesus, Jesus
It's like the ocean softly lapping on the shore.

Jesus, Jesus, Jesus,
It's like the whispering of the wind in trees.

Jesus, Jesus, Jesus,
It's like sheep grazing on a grassy hill.

Jesus, Jesus, Jesus,
It's the sound of rushes rustling by the riverside.

Jesus, Jesus, Jesus,
It's the unfolding petals of a rose.

Jesus, Jesus, Jesus,
It's the early murmuring of a summer's morn.

Jesus, Jesus, Jesus,
It's like a child singing as she skips.

Jesus, Jesus, Jesus,
It's like the rustling of your mother's skirt.

Jesus, Jesus, Jesus,
It's like your father sweeping leaves.

Jesus, Jesus, Jesus,
It's like footsteps on a shingle path.

Jesus, Jesus, Jesus,
It's the distant busyness of the day.

Jesus, Jesus, Jesus,
It's the purring of a cat cradled in loving arms.

Jesus, Jesus, Jesus,
It's the crunching of footsteps in fresh snow.

Jesus, Jesus, Jesus,
It's the singing silence of an empty church.

Jesus, Jesus, Jesus,
It's a sighing and a sleeping and a dying….

Jesus, Jesus, Jesus,
It's the voice I long to hear…

**Beloved child, Peace be with you.
I am here.**

Jesus, Jesus, Jesus.

AKP. November 1993

20

The Birth of a Son.

It happened thirty-three years ago... and yet...
... it seems like yesterday.
There he was at last... my baby... .a son...
He and I were alone for a few minutes...
No-one else was there.
I didn't have to share him... yet...

I remember...
I picked him up and held him close...
I felt his strong little body close to mine...
Just a short while ago he had been cocooned inside me.
Now he was a separate small person.

What would be his future?... I wondered...
I gazed at his face still crumpled from the birth-struggle...
I tucked my cheek close to his... and felt his warmth...
I felt the softness of his dark hair... now dry and soft...
Soft as thistledown...
As soft and dark as a baby duckling...

I whispered his name...

I looked at his hands... like little starfish...
Spread out... and perfect...
Each finger... each tiny finger-nail... perfect... a wonder...
How perfect!
I put my finger into his hand
And his fingers curled tightly around my finger.
Such a strong grip! What strength!
He held me as I held him...

And his feet...?
He thrust his feet out of the shawl... such strong legs...
How strong...!
And his feet...?
I held them in one hand.
He pushed his feet against my hand.
Tiny pink heels... perfect pink toes...
How wonderful!

I thought, "For these few moments he is mine, totally mine."
He opened his eyes and gazed up at me…
Our first shared look.
His eyes were dark and deep with knowing
We shared a long… deep… gaze…
Already we had shared so much.
How much more would we share?…
How much…?

But then I became conscious of noise and movement.
The world was beginning to crowd in on us.
I hugged him close to me… and knew
I had to start letting him go…
Letting him go.
So soon…?

AKP. November 2002

22

How would this world be

If Christ had never come?
The candle never lit
No beginning and no end of it.
A curtain never drawn
The play unveiled
In static silence left
A world bereft.

How would this world be
If Christ had never come?
A cake, uneaten, mouldering to a crumb
No light, no joy, no love, no peace.

How would that world be?
A child unborn
A joy unknown
A candle never lit
No journey – and no returning home.
No laughter caught
No cutting of the tree
A song unsung
A bell unrung
A world bereft.
No flower, no seed.

How would that world be?
No freedom and yet free
Unleashed in space
No place to go
No glory, Lord, to see.
No light, no joy, no love, no peace…
No point in living, Lord,
From dust to dust
And nothing in between….

BUT the glory of the Lord was seen
The acorn grew, the tree was green
The light was lit and shone

The darkness never was the same again.
The eternal flame burns on
And by its light we travel on
With light, with joy, with love and peace
Towards a better and a brighter place.

Then Glory be to God on High
"Onward and upward" is our cry.
In Christ we trust.

His promises He'll keep
And we awake at last to Him.
Will never want to sleep.
Praise and thanks to God
For all the gifts He's given
We'll do our stint on earth below
Before we go to Heaven.

AKP. December 1991

The Paralysed Man

Mute and anonymous,
passive and still,
with no story of his own to tell,
he was borne and offered
in the fiercely determined love
of stalwart companions.

At Your feet,
with nothing but his helplessness,
so few words were needed.

Forgiven, without question or reproach
with grace beyond imagining
and brought to wholeness.

New life for the taking, not for the earning
Life for the living, life for the running
Unshackled and ransomed
By Your extravagant love.

MT. January 2006

A Fir Cone of Forgiveness

Unforgiving, I hold myself together tightly
In shuttered seclusion,
Safe against further knocks and hurts.
The debris of past wrongs clings to me,
Choking my pores,
Enclosing me in a dull mantle of imprisoned safety.
Rendering me featureless and wizened,
As I protect my crumbling core.

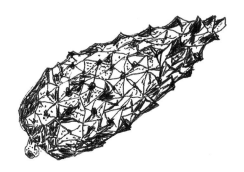

Open to God's forgiveness, I release my own forgiveness,
Warmed in his love
Light and lightness penetrate my core,
So that free and unburdened,
I proudly show the marks of my creator,
The fruit of His harvest.

MT. October 2003

26

Douglas

Douglas was my cross
He did not mean to be
But neither did the tree
O wounded, broken,
useless thing,
Exposed to all…
But Jesus set me free!
Alleluia!

AKP.1989

The Lantern Goblet

You set the goblet of your word before me,
Finely wrought, chased in gold and amber,
Bead-bubbling with sweet nectar of life and light.

Its honeyed fragrance draws me to its brim
Inviting me to taste, drink deep
Immerse my senses in its riches.

Each sip entices me to draw deeper
To quench my parched soul
until a warmth steals over me
And thirst and satisfaction mingle
In profound contentment.

Revived and replenished I rest in your radiance
Aglow with your redemptive promise
Racing thoughts stilled
Fears allayed
All other longings banished
Enfolded in your perfect peace.

MT. April 2006

28

The Moment

Alone and bathed in the light
The sound of trickling water
Runs over the rawness of my mind
Eroding the tyranny and pain of the past
And quenching my thirst for the future,
With the completeness of the moment.

A light pulse tingles through my limbs
Immersing me in gentle warmth.
The hard edges of my being melt away,
Until only my essential self remains
Light and malleable
In the hands of God
Moulding me in this most vibrant moment.

MT. September 2003

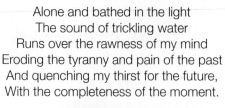

God makes all things new

Lured by the promise of a new creation
I offered myself, world wearied, sin stained
into His hands.

He drew me out of the shadows
Where I had grown inflexible and stale
Into the surrendering fire of His furnace
To be melted, moulded, purified, re-worked.
And there He forged the mysteries of His love
Healing fractured faith, distilling doubts,
Cleansing and refreshing my stubborn spirit.

And in the freshness of a new morning, He set me down,
unshackled and unburdened,
to step lightly and taste the freedom of a new beginning
with singing heart and mind uncluttered.
I saw his promise, with unmisted eyes
And found replenishment in still, clear air.

He gifted me with stillness
And bade me be,
Simply be ~ for His delight, His purpose
His new creation.

MT. April 2005

30

Under a Sussex Sky

Under a Sussex sky I was born
Beneath the bosom of the Downs I was nurtured.
As the breeze ripples across the pastures
As the tiny flowers nestle in the short Downland grass
So I was cared for and loved.

Beneath the white cliffs the sea
In all its changing beauty and fury is there.
Calm and sparkling in the summer sun,
Raging and wild in the autumn storms,
Cold and grey in mid-winter
But always there.

And the sun, rising in all its glory
Whatever the month or season,
Whether hidden by storm clouds or morning mist
Climbing in growing brilliance over the rim of the sea
The sun is there.
So it is with God.
Seen or unseen
God is always present.

And as the warmth of the sun invades the world
So it is with God's love,
A constant love.
Despite the clouds or storms, or times of darkness,
Deeper and more mysterious than the sea,
Lighter and more gentle than the warm fragrance
That breathes across the Downs on a summer's day
So it was and is and will be
God's precious love for you and me.

AKP. January 2004

I am a pot

Finished or not
Maybe a jug
Able to pour
But first I am made
Moulded and tested
Fired and rested
Then I can serve
My Maker.

Here I am
Unable to move
Unless I am moved
Unable to pour
Unless I am filled
Unless I am lifted
By my Maker.

Here is the pot
Or is it a jug?
No voice of its own
Unless it is gifted
No practical use
Unless it is lifted
But always forever
Whatever may be
A witness still
To the indelible skill
Of the Maker.

AKP. August 1990

33

No Other Way...

Before me stood
A barrier high and wide.
No other way for me to go
But down…
To crawl in comical awkwardness
And squeeze beneath the fence…
But ,oh, what joy…
When nose to ground,
I wriggled thro'
And found myself…
At Jesus' feet.

and found myself at Jesus' feet,

It was a lesson in humility…
For it is plain
For all to see
There is too much of me!
To make the passage
Through that space
Needs total loss of self…
But most of all
God's Grace.

AKP. 1995

Two Pictures and a Choice

I see a valley ,
deep and lush
where every tree
and every bush
is crowded with leafy green.

A river busies itself
beneath the trees
and between
the tops of wooded hills
is just a patch of sky.

I know the place.

But then…
I see another scene…

A rowan tree stands there
beside the stream
aged by the mountain frosts
and twisted by the wind
and yet its crown of berries
shine and glisten in the sun.

The stream murmurs
a Taize song
as it trickles
into the stillness
of the pool
beneath the old stone bridge.
The waters swirl down
to the silent deep.
The surface still
reflects the sky
and distant hill.

A timeless moment...
and then the stream
continued on its way
around rocky outcrops
and past peaty banks.

And all around
the moor stretches
fold on fold
into the heathered horizon.

No sound
but the constant murmur
of the stream,
the rasping
of a single grazing sheep
and the whisper of the wind.

Above, a sky
cerulean blue,
high and wide
billows with puffy clouds.
Their silent shadows
glide beneath.

The air breathes
gently across the scene
and whispers
to those who are there to hear...

" Keep the vision wide and clear.
Cast off the busy trappings
collected on the way.
Seek the silence
and stay
long enough
to be refreshed
and renewed
in the mystery of the deep
before you journey on."

AKP. November 1995

No Mountains here...

No mountains here... but only clouds.
No lakes here... but only puddles.
No rivers here... but only water running down the drain.
No God here...
Is there...?

There is. God is...
God is here.

God is in the light that brightens up the clouds...
In the reflection in the puddles...
In the cleansing as the water rushes down the drain...
God is.
God is in our breathing...in...and...out.
God is here.

AKP. September 2004

In azure waters...

In azure waters warm and deep
I swam with undulating grace
Free and supple
In liquid movement
In a limpid world.
Between cliffs of coral
And accompanied by You...
And a thousand little fish
Of rainbow colours
And glistening scales.
Such freedom and such joy was new to me.
How could I swim deep in a tranquil ocean
And be so at home....
And be so free...?

AKP. January 2005

40

Down woodland paths

Down woodland paths
in dappled sunlight
I danced with You.
Out to the meadows
bright with fragrant flowers
I danced with You.

Over the hillside
in perfect time
in perfect step
on and on we danced
just You and I.

So where shall we meet again?
And when?
Soon…
Soon…
Soon…

AKP May 2005

Light and dark

Deep in the mountains
the lake was still.
In a circle of silver water
a boat rocked gently
and I was in the boat
… in the light.
Rippled rings ran to the shore.
High on one side a dark precipice rose skywards
and sun gleamed in patches
moving across the green hills
to the distance.
Light and dark.
Calm, still, silver water
and rippled rings…
high black cliffs
and distant dappled hills
and I was in the boat with You.

AKP. August 2005

42

A Blessing for the Bruised

Amidst the quiet green cloisters of the garden
I saw the hand of the Celestial Architect
and stopped in wonder.

Birds tumbled their creation joys into the silence,
while fragrant blooms whispered their scented promises
on the rising air,
drawing me to drown my senses
in their fragrant hearts.

Each tender velvet petal inviting me to read
a private prayer in its creators praise.

And from my heart the heaviness fell away
and painful memories fled the corridors of my mind.

So bathed in the warming balm of sunlight,
I found a blessing for the bruised.

MT. June 2006

Catharsis

Haunted by tho raw and jagged memories of a darker time,
while we rehearsed the pain of our shared hurt,
we came upon the scene by chance.

At first unseeing and uncomprehending
we clambered doggedly through the labyrinthine maze of devastation.
The Hansel and Gretel wood of childhood games
laid waste before the scything fury of a winter storm.

Energy spent, we stopped and rested on an uprooted victim,
A fallen stalwart of former times.
So we, the veterans of another war,
Gazed in voiceless incredulity at ravaged landscape.

Trees ripped from their loamy wombs, spilled like discarded matchwood,
lay in undignified rest, as far as we could see.
Around their roots, now rudely exposed, clung signs of new life.
Pale shoots of bulbs, prematurely plucked,
and left to bloom or wither by unheeding midwife forces.

Locked in speechless thought, we pondered on the cries
that must have rent the air that terrible day.
What sounds of battle fury,
what groans and wails of agony among the fallen had gone unheard?

Now, in the heart of the still battleground,
full-throated birdsong salved the air in psalmody,
offering a valediction for the fallen.
And our battle weary souls found solemn sweet catharsis.

MT. May 2007

46

Amy K Perry and Margaret Thomas

Amy Perry, born in Sussex and brought up in a village in North Essex during the Second World War has lived in Burghfield Common, Berkshire for the last 42 years. She and her husband were married in 1963 and have a daughter and a son. Their son, Douglas , is severely mentally handicapped . Brain damage was caused through the late diagnosis of Phenylketonuria (PKU).

In the early 1980s Amy worked with Churches Together in Burghfield. After Amy retired from teaching in 1990 she gave more time to working in the local parish under the guidance of the Rector of Burghfield. In 1999, she was accepted for training as a Reader (Licensed Lay Minister) in the Anglican Church and was licensed in 2001. She was involved in the Christian Ministry of Prayer and Healing from the late 1980s.

The illustrations in this book are by Amy. After 1980 she renewed her interest in painting, especially watercolours, believing that God gave us gifts, which we should share for the joy, comfort and encouragement of fellow travellers through the ups and downs of life's journey.

Margaret was born in Manchester in 1946 and was brought up against the backdrop of industrial cotton mills. On leaving school she did a degree in English at Swansea University, where she met her future husband, Brian.

After their marriage in 1968, they moved to Burghfield Common in Berkshire, where she taught in local schools, raised her own family and immersed herself in Church and village life. Like Amy, she became interested in the Christian Ministry of Healing and is a lay member of the ministry of healing team in her local village church. Retirement, though busy, has brought the opportunity to write, garden and explore issues of faith through poetry. Currently she helps to lead Emmaus groups in her local church and is keen to encourage people to discover the playful and creative side of their natures by exploring the scriptures through poetry and art.

Amy and Margaret have been friends since the 1970s and have supported each other through the ups and downs in life. They worked together, professionally, teaching in the local primary school , and served together working in many aspects in the church and the parish of Burghfield. After sharing their poems with each other in the last few years they decided to publish their poems and Amy's illustrations which she has created over the years.

48

Notes

The Garden Poems

The Gardener

Written in June 2004 this was inspired by a quiet day at Oak House Quiet Garden, when we were invited to reflect on the garden of our lives.

The Rose

June 2005, at another Oak House day, my eye was caught by a simple arrangement of old roses in a bowl.

God with me

Written in April 2004 this piece was inspired by reading Isaiah 30. Verse 18 tells us "The Lord longs to be gracious to you… blessed are all who wait for him!"

Warmth in Winter

Before the Fire

Written on the Advent Quiet Day in December 2002 on the day of my daughter's scan on her twin babies. It had been discovered earlier in the week that one of the babies appeared to be rather poorly, and that the scan would hopefully shed more light on the problem. All I could do was hand my fears over to the Lord.

Next Year's Poppies

Written in December 2004. Two years on and at another Advent Quiet Day. It was the close of a dreadful year for the family. One of our twin grandsons had lost his fight for life on New Year's Day 2004. Relationships foundered in the aftermath and I found myself very much a "hands on" grandmother spending half of each week in Sussex caring for my remaining grandson, while my newly single daughter went back to work. The green shoots of poppies and the flickering of candles through a misted window gave me hope that next year might bring better things.

Dark Times

The Open Wound

Written on the 12th November 1992 just after the vote in General Synod on the Ordination of Women. As I watched the debate in the afternoon, I was deeply aware of the pain felt by one bishop as he spoke against the motion. That night I dreamed of a huge red open wound and in the morning wrote about my vision in a poem. The poem and illustration come from my journal.

Besieging Spirit

A Quiet Day on the subject of prayer in July 2004 was the springboard for this poem. Much of our difficulty in our prayer life stems from our refusal to draw on the Holy Spirit. By allowing the Holy Spirit space to pray within us and intercede for us, we are relieved of our own limited prayer agenda and are free to receive all that the Lord longs to give us.

Hollow

This was written in the early autumn of 2005. This was another difficult year for the family. Members of every generation seemed beset by problems of one kind or another. I found myself stretched very thinly as I travelled between family members giving what help I could.

Psalm for Today

Written in December 1995 at a time when I was feeling depressed. I decided to read the psalms. Meditating on Psalm 27 I felt determined that I was not going to give way to all that was raining down on me at that time. The poem and accompanying somewhat comic illustration was the result of that resolve.

Care and Prayer

In Intensive Care

When a dear member of our church was suddenly rushed into intensive care there was great distress at Church. Many rallied to pray, and soon we had a prayer chain that stretched across continents, right round the world, so that prayers for him were offered throughout 24 hours. Two of us visited his wife as she kept vigil at the hospital and we were invited to visit him in the ICU. I had never been in such a place before. Struck by the quiet, save for the whirring of machines, I was able to place my hand on him as I prayed. When I came away, the key question on my mind was "Where is his soul?" I wrote this poem on the 4th August 1995 and shared it with those who were praying for him. Many said how helpful they found it. Our friend almost died on three occasions, but recovered and was gradually restored to full health.

Watch and Pray

In the summer of 1991 I walked alongside another friend during her struggle with terminal cancer. At one point we attended a Christian healing service together. When she deteriorated and was taken to hospital, she was not allowed visitors. I found this distressing and it was hard to pray at a distance. I thought of the friends of Jesus who had stood beneath his cross feeling helpless. All they could do was watch and pray.
This poem was the result of those thoughts.
I was later given a postscript!   Jesus would forgive us if we felt we had failed in our efforts to watch and pray.

Meditations

After the Rain

Written in 2005 as I sat in the summerhouse of Oak House Garden on a chilly wet morning just prior to Easter, meditating on Mark 14 v 37.

Jesus, Jesus, Jesus

A dear friend was going through a difficult patch. Many family members and friends at the time were suffering distress and looking to her for comfort. I offered her this poem hoping it would help to soothe her troubled soul.

Meditation on the Birth of a Son

First published in The Door, the monthly newspaper of the Oxford Diocese, December 2004. Margaret and I were co-leading an Advent course. We planned to spend a session on each of the central characters in the story of Jesus' birth. As I meditated on the Virgin Mary and her motherhood, I realised that my son, Douglas, was 33 and so the same age our Lord was thought to be when he was crucified. I wondered how much Mary would remember in her later years of the birth of her first son.

When I thought of the birth of my son, I could remember how I felt, how I had examined him very closely as we had shared those first few intimate moments and how, as a mother, I had wondered what his future would be.

My perfect baby was later to suffer brain damage. I have learned a great deal through my son and the experiences I have had because of him.

How would this world be?

In December 1991, one of my uncles died. His funeral was held on Christmas Eve and naturally this made Christmas a sad time. In the middle of the night on December 28th these thoughts came to me and I found them uplifting. What a wonderful difference Jesus' coming had made to the whole world, whether we recognise him or not.

The Paralysed Man

I had been asked to lead a meditation on Mark 2 1-12, for our church's Service of Christian Healing in January 2006. Spending quiet time with this vivid and familiar story, which had captured my imagination as long ago as Sunday school, these first thoughts came to me.

Grace...Shafts of Light

A Fir Cone of Forgiveness

This was written during a very quiet Quiet Day at our Parish Centre (just 3 of us attended!). After a time of relaxation and meditation, we were dispatched to the churchyard to find something to add to a beautiful focal point that had been prepared by our visiting leader. The theme for the day was forgiveness – God's forgiveness and our own attempts at forgiveness. Somewhat idly, I mooched around the fallen autumn debris. I began to gather a collection of fir cones, as I had so often done as a child. Would this rather grubby uninspired collection serve as my contribution? God, as ever, was just longing for me to have an "idle" moment, so He could get a word in!

Douglas

This poem was written in 1989 when Douglas was 20.
When Douglas was born, I had stopped going to church, thinking I could do without God. Gradually over the years, I came back to faith. Having a mentally handicapped son was very difficult and I had felt bowed down under the burden. This poem was a shout of joy as I had come to believe that Jesus was the saviour of all of us, Douglas included.

The Lantern Goblet

In the dying light of a quiet winter afternoon, a candle burning in a pretty glass goblet, glimpsed through half closed eyes brought a flash of radiant peace.

The Moment

At the time of writing this poem, I was very concerned about what the future held for my desperately poorly grandson. At a Quiet Day at The Oak House Garden I found the answers I had been looking for in Matthew 6 v 25 – 34. The same day I was also recommended Eckhart Tolle's remarkable book, The Power of Now. For anyone finding them self living in the rose tinted memories of the past or straining to see what the future might hold, it is a liberating read!

God makes all things new

This poem was the fruits of another Quiet Day at The Oak House garden in April 2005. Its inspiration came from meditating on 2 Corinthians 5 v 17 "Anyone who is joined to Christ is a new being; the old is gone, the new has come."

Under a Sussex Sky

Even before Margaret's twin grandsons were born, we were involved in praying for them, step by step as the early scans of the pregnancy showed all was not well with baby Oscar. We continued to pray through Oscar's first months, through his trials and joys. He died on New Year's Day 2004 and I helped Margaret and her family with suggestions in planning his funeral. I too was born in Sussex, nurtured in the bosom of the Downs, and know how close the presence of God is for all of us through that landscape's changing seasons.

Visions and Dreams

I am a Pot

I was meditating on Jeremiah 18 v 1-6 when this poem started to form itself in my mind. The poem dates from August 1990. When my son Douglas collapsed and was rushed into hospital, very close to death, I read this poem as I visited him each day. It gave me the courage to believe that I was being moulded and tested in God's hands and prepared for his use. I was also given the assurance that Douglas would recover.

No other way

I was praying, the day before I was due to take part in a service of Christian Healing at the Vine in Caversham, when a picture came into my mind. I saw a huge barrier, which reached up as far as I could see. Looking down, I saw a tiny crack at the bottom. Looking through, I could see something on the other side, but was not sure what it was. I crawled through the small opening and found myself looking at the feet of Jesus! I was very aware what a comical sight I looked and realised I was being taught a lesson in humility!

Two Pictures and a Choice

I followed a course on prayer in November 1995. At the time I was uncertain about where I was in my spiritual life and what I should be doing. Two pictures came to me. The first scene I recognised as Moretonhamstead Golf Course, the second was of a high open place in mid Wales. The scenes reflected my choices, an easy way or the road through a more barren landscape.

No Mountains Here

Whenever I return from holidaying in Austria, I always feel sad and have to make do with clouds for the mountains I miss so much.

A Trilogy

I attended three sessions of soaking prayer in 2005 and each time received a very different experience. The first two, In Azure Waters and Down Woodland Paths were beautiful, but the third, Light and Dark had a much darker side to it and was actually a forewarning of spiritually difficult times ahead. All three have been of great comfort to me as I have re-read them and meditated on what I have received.

Peace after the Storms

A Blessing for the Bruised

This poem was written in June 2006. It was a difficult time for many in our church, and I took my inspiration from reading Elijah's story. Elijah knew incredible highs, but also plumbed the depths of depression and fear. Flawed as he was God used him to powerful effect and his doggedly persistent prayers turned his fears to faith and his doubts to certainty. So I hoped it would be for us bruised ambassadors for the Lord.

Catharsis

A walk over our local common took a dramatic turn when Amy and I realised the full extent of the devastation wreaked by the storms of January 2007. We had seen a number of dear friends go through stormy times over the previous few months, sharing their pain and dilemmas and seeing the victims of this woodland storm had deep resonances for both of us.